BEAR MARKETS AND BEYOND

A BESTIARY OF BUSINESS TERMS

BY DHRUTI SHAH AND DOMINIC BAILEY

WELCOME TO THE JUNGLE

Unicorns, narwhals, yaks, cows and civets – what have all these creatures got to do with your hard-earned cash? Well, far more than you might think at first glance.

They are all beasts that appear in the global economic ecosystem. They pop up as warnings, messages and signals and provide us with useful analogies for describing and navigating what can sometimes be a confusing, closed-off world.

Animals have always exerted a strong hold on our imagination. You only have to look at prehistoric cave paintings to see how central they were to our existence and, in capturing these images and using them to pass on messages to the community, we can see how they were our first linguistic tools and shaped our relationship with each other.

It's therefore not surprising that, many millennia later, our contemporary Capitalist world is populated with metaphorical animals that stalk the landscape and alert us in the same way to what we can trust and what we should fear.

Indeed, according to John Maynard Keynes, perhaps the most influential economist of the last century, we are all in the sway of Animal Spirits. We may think that our behaviour, especially when dressed in a sharp-tailored business suit, is governed by facts and logic and the rationale of a well-reasoned argument. However, Keynes begs to differ and says, in his 1936 text on *The General Theory of Employment, Interest and Money:*

'Most, probably, of our decisions to do something positive, the full consequences of which will be drawn out over many days to come, can only be taken as the result of animal spirits – a spontaneous urge to action rather than inaction, and not as the outcome of a weighted average of quantitative benefits multiplied by quantitative probabilities.'

And so, as we find ourselves in the financial jungle, a place of intense competition, where the rules are simply; survival of the fittest, we hope this guide will be your friend. The jargon of the business world is a code but we're on hand to crack it. You wouldn't want to enter a bear pit unprepared, so watch out for the big beasts baring their teeth and keep your wits about you as you follow us through the undergrowth...

ALLIGATOR

ALLIGATOR SPREAD

The financial world is full of predators hoping to climb their way to the top of the food chain, so it's unsurprising that reptiles make an early appearance in our guide.

In the world of markets, an Alligator Spread occurs when an investor will never be able to make a profit on the transactions they make. This is because the charges of the commissions involved are far higher than the profit made. The spread thus 'eats the investor', leading to the name Alligator Spread.

ALLIGATOR PROPERTY

Take a quick wander over to the property market and you find that landlords need to take care that they don't invest in an Alligator Property. That's when the costs of investing in and running a property far exceeds any profits derived from the rental. That house, which you thought would be your nest egg (see p. 110), could actually end up eating all your money.

ANT

Did you know that ants can carry between ten and fifty times their own body weight? Pretty impressive. However, you've got to be very careful if you ever get described as an 'ant' in China.

Chinese officials are using the term to describe people who take Chinese money and carry it across borders and overseas. The government is worried about this capital flight and has been cracking down on it.

BAT

—

BAT PHONE

Named after the direct hotline Gotham City's Commissioner Gordon has to DC Comics' superhero, Batman, the Bat Phone is only for the upper echelons of the trading universe. It's a tightly guarded private telephone number for high priority calls. Strictly for insiders.

BEAR

Bears pop up a lot in business and nobody is quite clear on why they are such a feature of the financial landscape, though some claim it is because The London Stock Exchange was set up in the seventeenth century, a time when bear-baiting was a popular pastime.

BEAR INVESTORS

Bear investors target vulnerable securities and try to make a profit from a decline in stock prices. Many believe it all goes back to the old bearskin traders and the idiom 'to sell the bear's skin before one has caught the bear'. This was when the middleman or 'bearskin jobber' would sell a skin at one price and then buy it cheaper from the trapper, pocketing the profit.

BEAR MARKET

This goes straight to the heart of the stock echanges. Whilst the value of stocks generally rise and fall, at times they simply fall and fall. And if you have a fall of twenty per cent or a long-term decline of more than two months, this is when you have a Bear Market. It is the opposite of a Bull Market (see p.26), some believe this pairing dates back to when bulls and bears were pitted against each other in staged fights. The bull would thrust its horns upwards, while the bear would swat down with its paws.

BEES

KILLER BEES

Killer Bees aren't necessarily as scary as you might think. They refer to the firms or individuals who help a company that has been targeted with a hostile takeover bid. They include investment bankers, accountants, lawyers and tax specialists and their defence strategies are usually to make the company look less appealing or profitable and therefore less easy to acquire.

QUEEN BEE

The term Queen Bee was coined in 1973 by psychologists from the University of Michigan. It describes a woman who, in a position of authority in a male-dominated environment, views and treats female subordinates in a more critical manner.

However, the original researchers have said that they now hate the term and that their findings were more about the sexist atmosphere in place at the time of their work. A lot of subsequent research has gone on to suggest that women do support each other in the workplace.

BIRD

—

BIRD DOG

If you're particularly risk-averse, perhaps a career as a Bird Dog may suit. That's the name given to someone who spends ages researching the market and hunting down properties they think are worth investing in. They then pass on the leads to the actual investors (so they're purely a middle man).

BIRD-IN-HAND THEORY

This comes from the well-known adage, 'A bird in the hand is worth two in the bush' and, put simply, advises you to value what you have rather than what you don't possess.

The idiom has also been used by economists Myron Gordon and John Lintner, whose Bird-in-Hand Theory suggests that investors prefer getting consistent dividends from their stocks rather than betting on capital gains. The latter can give investors a far more substantial financial reward and yet their risky nature makes them far less attractive than stocks which offer the prospect of regular, reliable dividends.

BIRDS OF PREY

EAGLES

This acronym was created by the Spanish bank BBVA in 2010 and stands for Emerging and Growth-Leading Economies.

The criteria for membership is countries 'whose contribution to world economic growth in the following ten years is expected to be larger than the average of the leading industrialised nations, namely the G6 countries'. Initially, the list included the BRIC countries of Brazil-Russia-India-China, and also South Africa, South Korea, Indonesia, Mexico, Turkey, Egypt and Taiwan (see page 38).

While BBVA did, for a number of years, issue an annual report about the Eagles and their futures, it stopped doing so in 2016, instead choosing to focus on publishing reports on specific issues affecting emerging economies.

Does this mean the term is dead as a dodo? Not necessarily...

HAWK

A Hawk is a policymaker or adviser who tends to put a high priority on curbing inflation and is more willing than a Dove (see below) to see higher interest rates used as a means to achieve it.

DOVE

A Dove is a policymaker or adviser who tends to be less willing than a Hawk to see higher interest rates used to curb inflation.

VULTURE INVESTOR

A Vulture Investor will invest in distressed firms, assets or bonds in the hope that, after buying at a steep discount, there will be a turnaround and the vulture can profit from this.

They often buy from those who are desperate to sell and don't have a lot of buyers to choose from. However, the typical vulture strategy is to mine the value of their investment and use legal routes to take ownership of the company's assets – and then potentially break that company up.

There is also a shadier side to Vulture Investing which involves the purchase in government bonds or debts of struggling developing countries. Bonds are bought at a deeply discounted price and then, subsequently, investment firms have been known to take legal action to demand full payment. Argentina, Peru, Venezuela, Zambia and many others have all been on the receiving end of this kind of action.

VULTURE FUND

A Vulture Fund invests in companies or countries that are struggling, or that are very risky, in the hope of making huge profits should they recover.

BULL

BULL MARKET

A Bull Market is the opposite of a Bear Market (see p.14). Some believe the analogy originates from the bull-and-bear fights of the eighteeth century. A bull attacks by thrusting its horns upwards, so when the price of shares on the stock market is rising, it's a 'bull market'.

In fact, anything that is traded (bonds, real estate, currencies and commodities), can be described as a bull market when the trend is upwards. The trajectory has to be fairly sustained so, typically, the rise in stock prices is ongoing and market confidence is high.

BUTTERFLY

IRON BUTTERFLY

An Iron Butterfly is a limited-risk, limited-profit trading strategy. It occurs when an investor puts themselves in a protected situation, whatever happens with the market, and is referred to colloquially as an 'Iron Fly'. The investor engages in this sort of trade because it will make them a nice bit of money if they are correct in believing that markets are becoming less volatile.

CAMEL

VOMITING CAMEL

This gross-sounding beast first emerged in 2014 through the wonderful world of Twitter.

At one point, *Financial Times* journalist, Katie Martin's Twitter bio described herself as the 'founder and chief investment officer at Vomiting Camel Asset Management'. This, as you might have guessed, was a bit of a tongue-in-cheek role.

Some technical analysts like to spend their days looking for patterns in charts to figure out which way the market is heading. And in 2014, when finance worker Suvi Platerink posted a picture of her colleague's vision of a vomiting camel on a RDX (Russian Depositary Index) chart – believed to be the first sighting in the wild – the internet applauded. Martin started scribbling the camel in various charts she spotted, all the while admitting it was a joke. However, the camel soon took on a life of its own and weirdly, has been treated as a serious analytical tool on some media channels.

So if you spot a vomiting camel, maybe, just maybe take another look...

CATS

Cats turn up everywhere in business and often, as in life, where you least expect them.

BECKONING CAT (MANEKI-NEKO)

The Maneki-Neko may be a familiar sight to you. Many believe it comes from China but it's actually Japanese in origin. The name literally means 'Beckoning Cat' and it's a plastic or ceramic figurine with one paw raised and 'beckoning'. To Westerners, it often seems as if the cat is waving but this is because the Japanese gesture for beckoning differs and is performed by holding up the hand, palm down, and repeatedly folding the fingers, like the cat.

These cats are seen as a lucky charm, believed to bring success and prosperity, and so are displayed in shops and businesses. It is thought that cats with the left paw raised attract more customers, while cats with the right paw raised attract more money, so the former is traditionally for business and the latter is for the home. You also see these cats with both paws raised.

COPY-CAT

Whether you are starting out in the world of finance or you're already a massive player, you certainly never want to be a Copy-cat (unless you are operating in the world of fake goods) as either you could get sued or the market for the product you created could end up saturated and your profits disappear.

Although, saying that, sometimes entrepreneurs and companies will seek inspiration from each other and that explains why, when you see a town with one successful coffee shop, it soon starts playing host to a lot more.

DEAD CAT BOUNCE

Ever heard of a dead cat bounce? It's not as horrible as it sounds and means a temporary recovery in the price of a stock that's fallen significantly. It originated on Wall Street and comes from the idea that 'even a dead cat will bounce if you throw it from a tall enough height'.

Investors will look out for a sharp and sudden decline and then try to grab a bargain. However, this can cause the stock price to rally, yet not for long if the fundamentals that were responsible for the decline remain unchanged. Dead Cats tend to involve a weak bounce-back.

FAT CAT

Money problems rarely bother a Fat Cat. The label is often used to describe a rich and greedy person who owns lots of assets and uses the work of others to get even richer. It also refers to executives whose pay is perceived by others to be excessive.

The term is generally quite derogatory and, in the US, the slang phrase is also used to refer to wealthy people who make significant contributions to political parties and campaigns.

In 1928, the writer Frank Kent's essay 'Fat Cats and Free Rides', published in *The American Mercury*, painted a very vivid picture of the eponymous Fat Cat, stating, 'A Fat Cat is a man of large means and slight political experience who, having reached middle age, and success in business, and finding no further thrill, sense or satisfaction in the mere piling up of more millions, develops a yearning for some sort of public honor, and is willing to pay for it'.

CHICKEN

CHICKEN INVESTOR

Cluck, cluck, cluck – here you have a Chicken Investor.

The challenge with these domesticated birds is that they are deathly afraid – of everything. And chicken investors approach the market with the same kind of trepidation. They cluck around with no particular plan. They are spooked by any kind of loss and fear easily overrides common sense. But this means they never stand a chance to make any type of gain.

We've seen that the bulls get paired with the bears; well for some reason (perhaps the farmyard proximity), the chickens often seem to get paired with pigs (see p. 118).

CIVET

Now a civet is a small nocturnal mammal found in Asia and Africa. CIVETS, however, is the acronym that you get when you bundle Colombia, Indonesia, Vietnam, Egypt, Turkey and South Africa together.

Back in 2001, economist Lord O'Neill of Goldman Sachs coined the term BRIC to classify the heavyweight emerging economies of Brazil, Russia, India and China, and the term stuck. Later South Africa joined changing BRIC to BRICS.

Then, in 2008, Robert Ward,the Economist Intelligence Unit's global forecasting director came up with CIVETS, which identified another group of emerging markets to watch. In his eyes, all the countries listed above offered up 'large, young, growing' populations and 'diverse and dynamic economies'.

In 2018, Ward told the authors of this book: 'I wanted to draw attention to Tier 2 EMs (Emerging Markets), i.e. the level below the BRICS. Not that they've worn terribly well, especially Turkey of late.' At the time of writing, the markets have certainly been rather volatile and have not quite lived up to what the forecasters of 2008 onwards were expecting.

COCKROACH
—

COCKROACH PORTFOLIO

Cockroaches, it's said, can survive nuclear blasts and, whether this is strictly true or not, this reputation for resilience is highly attractive in the business world. When analyst Dylan Grice left Société Générale in 2012, he signed off his final Popular Delusions column by highlighting his ideal type of portfolio; the Cockroach Portfolio. The investments are divided between twenty-five per cent cash; twenty-five per cent government bonds; twenty-five per cent equities and twenty-five per cent gold, which means risk is spread and the portfolio is crash-proof, nuclear-proof even.

The founder of Flickr, Caterina Fake, also suggests that startups, which are 'creative about the products they build, smarter about who they hire and how the company spends its time', are the 'hardy cockroaches' that will survive apocalypses.

COCKROACH THEORY

Cockroaches are social creatures... so if you see one, watch out for its friends. In the same way, Cockroach Theory refers to the belief that, when a company reveals some bad news, it's likely that's not the last of it – there'll be more to follow.

COW

CASH COW

Now what everybody needs is a Cash Cow as this bovine is one that, like a dairy cow producing milk for many years, produces a steady flow of cash. Very little maintenance is required and, after the initial capital outlay has been paid off, you have a guaranteed income. Lovely. Some famous cash cows include Kellogg's Corn Flakes ®, Coca-Cola ® and Ford ® Transit vans.

SACRED COW

Mooving on... Cash Cows are the money makers but Sacred Cows are untouchable. They are organisations and individuals who can't be criticised in any way. The term also refers to beliefs that have become enshrined as received wisdom and are hard to independently verify, such as saving ten to fifteen per cent of your pay for retirement if you want an easier life.

In the seminal text *A Business and Its Beliefs*, IBM CEO Tom Watson Jr states: 'Beliefs must always come before policies, practices and goals. The latter must always be altered if they are seen to violate fundamental beliefs. The only sacred cow in an organisation should be its basic philosophy of doing business'.

CROCODILE

—

Crocodiles occupy an enviable position on the top rungs of the food chain – they are predator, not prey. And so China's financial regulators apply this reptilian term to individuals and conglomerates who are using aggressive tactics and unfairly profiteering from the stock market.

Additionally, many of China's multi-billion conglomerates, such as Wanda Group and Anbang Insurance Group, have been spending freely on high-(over)priced overseas acquisitions. In the regulators' eyes, they have been 'swimming across' the national border with Chinese money. They are not impressed, and have vowed to hunt these 'financial crocodiles'.

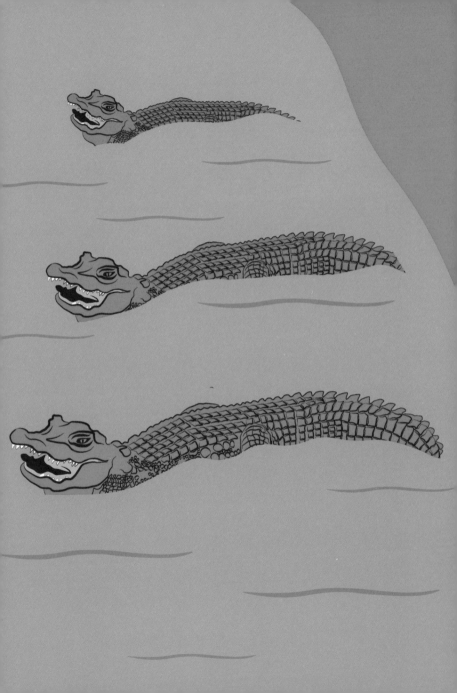

DEER

DEER MARKET

What if investors are holding off, too timid to make a move? Then, it's a Deer Market. It doesn't mean the market is in trouble, just nothing much is going on – so certainly no bunny-hopping here (see p. 126).

STAG

A Stag is an impatient investor. When a company goes public, it is listed on the stock exchange and shares are offered to be bought and sold. A Stag doesn't hang around to see how things pan out as they'll have bought shares prior to public trading and then sell them straight away. It's a strategy that is no-nonsense and fast-moving.

A Stag likes hot deals and quick profits. Oh Bambi, is this what you'll grow up to be?

DOGS

—

What about 'man's best friend'? Yes, dogs turn up in the world of business too.

BULLDOG BONDS

When foreign banks or firms want to raise money from investors in the UK in British Pounds Sterling, they may issue bulldog bonds.

It might be helpful here to break down what bonds actually are, so we turned to BBC World Service economics expert Andrew Walker to give us a general overview. He delivered and we learn 'in short it is an IOU that can be traded in the financial markets'.

Governments, official agencies and businesses can all sell bonds. Those who invest do so as they then get a stream of future payments.

When a firm is in need of foreign currency or anticipates favourable interest rates in a foreign market, they will choose that national bond market to trade in. Woof! (See also Dragon, Kangaroo, Kiwi and Panda Bonds, pp. 54, 86, 88 and 116.)

BULLDOG MARKET

An affectionate term for the UK's foreign bond market.

DOGECOIN

For a bit of surrealism, let's head to the world of cryptocurrencies and a very peculiar mascot. Dogecoin began as a parody currency with a logo that uses the infamous internet meme of a Shiba Inu dog named Kabosu.

Dogecoin was created by American Billy Markus and Australian Jackson Palmer and was launched in 2013 when bitcoin became all the rage. Whilst Palmer stresses that Dogecoin started as joke, at one point the digital currency reached a market capitalisation of $2 billion US dollars in January 2018, before sliding back down again.

What does its future actually hold? Elon Musk, the entrepreneur behind SpaceX, Tesla and Paypal did once tweet that Dogecoin was his favourite cryptocurrency but there are many economists who are sceptical of the long-term staying power of cryptocurrencies in general.
So who knows...?

DOG EAT DOG

Throughout your working life, it's probably best to steer clear of Dog Eat Dog behaviour. That's when it becomes a matter of the survival of the fittest (we're seeing this theme pop up a lot). That's when people are willing to harm each other in order to succeed. Not a nice concept at all.

DOGS OF THE DOW

Dogs of the Dow is an investment strategy made popular by money manager Michael B. O'Higgins. The idea is that you look at the Dow Jones stock market index and then pick the ten stocks which have the highest dividend yields. As per the name, these types of stocks are also known as 'dogs' in Wall Street. Often it is businesses which are at their lowest share price that will have the highest dividend yield. But the plan is to then keep hold of these stocks in the hope their performance will pick up over the next year and you can then make a very tidy profit. As the Dow Jones is made up of blue chip companies – which are reputable, financially sound, established businesses – those who follow the strategy believe they will see solid returns.

DRAGON

—

As China's economy has gone from strength to strength, financiers now often refer to the country using the shorthand term, Dragon.

DRAGON BONDS

Dragon bonds, which are issued by Asian nations, are denominated in US dollars. They were introduced by the Asian Development Bank and are used to attract foreign investment. (See also Bulldog, Kangaroo, Kiwi and Panda Bonds, pp. 48, 86, 88 and 116.)

DRAGON-KINGS

You want to watch out for Dragon-Kings. Identified by risk specialist Professor Didier Sornette, he says they are extreme events but that 'they are generated by specific mechanisms that may make them predictable, perhaps controllable.' This contrasts with Black Swan Theory (see p. 146), which proposes the concept of unpredictable events. Sornette's theory involves many factors. Indeed, he stresses that Dragon-King events are 'special events associated with specific bubble regimes that precede them'. There is a lot going on beforehand.

DUCK

—

This poor bird makes for easy prey.

LAME DUCK

Lame Duck refers to an individual or company that cannot keep up with the rest of the market. The phrase was coined in the eighteeth century at the London Stock Exchange and referred to a stockbroker who defaulted on his debts. The *Oxford English Dictionary* cites the letters of English writer Horace Walpole in 1761 as the first recorded use, where he asks: 'Do you know what a Bull, and a Bear, and a Lame Duck are?'

Investors who continually make poor trades and lose out on profits are also described as Lame Ducks.

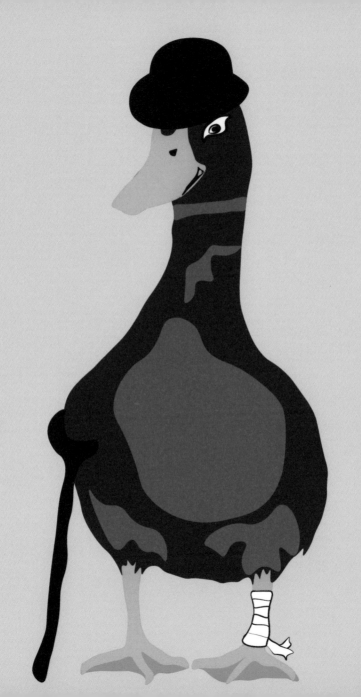

SITTING DUCK

A Sitting Duck refers to an individual or business that doesn't have a lot of protection and is vulnerable to attack.

UGLY DUCKLING STOCKS

Ugly Duckling Stocks are those that are underperforming but that are also seen by speculative investors as having the potential for improvement and thus to be of value. Fund manager, Donald Yacktman, looks for bargains to invest in as he understands 'the transformation from the ugly duckling to the swan doesn't happen instantaneously'.

MILKSHAKE DUCK

A Milkshake Duck refers to an internet meme that stands for a person or thing that enjoys huge initial popularity, which is then followed by the revelation of flaws that make its popularity too problematic. The term has gained prominence in an era where cancel culture has derailed careers. People have lost jobs after becoming famous but then their social media history has been trawled through and it's been found they aren't the perfect person the internet initially deemed them to be.

ELEPHANT
—

ELEPHANT CURVE

On any animal safari, it's fascinating to see a pachyderm pop up and an Elephant Curve in the world of economics is no exception. It refers to the shape of the curve on a graph that reveals the effect of development on the distribution of income and was created by former World Bank economist Branko Milanovic and his colleague Christoph Lakner.

The graph shows the growth in real incomes across the world's income distribution between 1988 and 2008. The very richest, who are represented by the tip of the trunk did very well; while the very poorest (at the tail) did not. Some in the middle classes in Brazil, for example did see some strong gains. There has been some debate about what the dip means but it may be lower income groups in rich countries, or stagnating Japan and post-Soviet economies.

There was an effort to update the chart with a version focusing on the years 1980 to 2016 unveiled in the 2018 World Inequality Report. That version though was viewed by many to look like the Loch Ness Monster! The trunk had extended while the space where the elephant's head had been had shrunk...

ELEPHANT HUNTING

American business mogul and shrewd investor, Warren
Buffett, has said that when he's seeking large companies to
acquire, he refers to it as 'hunting the elephant'. Considering
he's one of the richest men in the world, it seems his
strategy has worked...

ELEPHANT OIL FIELDS

As we all know, oil is essential to our economies and so,
when an Elephant Oil Field appears, it generates a great
deal of excitement. Understandably, as these fields contain a
minimum of 500 million barrels of oil. The term is a generic
one but it's also an alternative name for Libya's El Feel Field.

WHITE ELEPHANT

White elephants were magnificent creatures. So rare in
occurance that they were instantly gifted to the monarchs
of countries such as Laos, Myanmar, Thailand and Cambodia.
However, as they were considered sacred they couldn't be
used for labour and were rather expensive to look after.

This explains why, in the world of business, a White Elephant
refers to an unprofitable investment and probably isn't a
good thing to have in your portfolio of holdings. It can also
be a project or any other high-maintenance possession that
gives you very little return.

FISH

—

BOTTOM FISHING

Sometimes, when traders try to time that Dead Cat Bounce we mentioned earlier (see p. 33), they'll end up in the realm of Bottom Fishing. This is when they invest in cheap, undervalued stocks in the anticipation that the market will rally.

CATFISH

In the modern world, you want to be careful that you don't become the victim of a Catfish. A Catfish creates a fake online identity to try to defraud others. Sometimes, they'll even steal identities, so watch out.

FISH SCALES

What do fish scales have to do with money? Well, Czech traditions dictate that, if you put a carp fish scale in your wallet at Christmas time, it could bring you prosperity in the New Year.

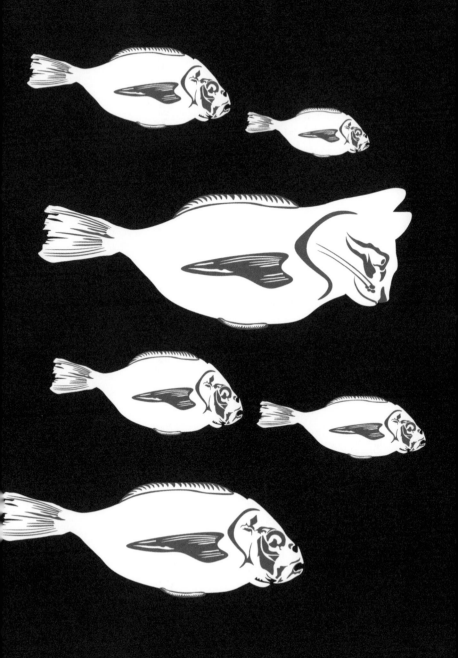

FISHBONE ANALYSIS

Fishbone Analysis is a cause-and-effect diagram for tracing any problems, challenges or defects in how something is designed back to the root cause. It was created by organisational theorist Kaoru Ishikawa and it looks just like a fishbone. The defect is the fish's head, while the causes are the fishbones, with major causes represented by the ribs.

RED HERRING

The phrase 'Red Herring' commonly refers to a piece of information that's intended to be misleading. The first usage seems to go back to 1807, with *Cobbett's Weekly Political Register* as its source point.

A Red Herring can also be the legal document that a company files with the US Securities and Exchange Commission in connection with its initial public offering. However, as a prospectus, it doesn't include key details and the name refers to its disclaimer, printed in red ink, which states that the registration has yet to be made effective.

SLIPPERY FISH

A Slippery Fish is someone who is clever and deceitful.

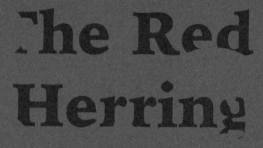

FLEA MARKET

—

A Flea Market is where lots of second-hand goods are sold. It's a translation of the French *Marché aux puces* in Paris.

In 1922, American writer George S. Dougherty wrote in his book *In Europe* that 'it is called the "Flea" Market because there are so many second-hand articles sold of all kinds that they are believed to gather fleas'.

This is starting to make us feel a bit itchy...

FROG

—

BOILED FROG THEORY

Ever heard of the Boiled Frog Theory? Well, a frog is a cold-blooded creature and so, when you put him in a pot of cold water and turn the heat up, his temperature will keep adjusting as the water temperature rises. However, when the water is about to reach boiling point, the frog can't adjust anymore and so he tries to jump out. But he can't.

Let's be clear, this is not based on any real-life frog experiment (as far as our research can ascertain – and nor would we condone any type of animal cruelty). Rather, the Nobel Laureate economist and journalist, Paul Krugman, used this metaphor in a now-very-famous *New York Times* opinion piece to explain some of the problems the American economy was facing in 2009.

Krugman states: 'The hypothetical boiled frog is a useful metaphor for a very real problem: the difficulty of responding to disasters that creep up on you a bit at a time'.

GADFLY

This little insect makes its presence known by biting and annoying livestock. Similarly, in the business world, this small irritant is a shareholder who attends AGMs (Annual General Meetings), asks provocative questions and challenges the status quo, thus highlighting bad management and lobbying for change.

GAZELLE

A Gazelle Company is a term, devised by economist David Birch, which refers to young and very fast-growing companies whose sales double every four years.

GOLD BUG

In the world of finance, a Gold Bug is an investor who is bullish about gold and believes in it both as a commodity and also as a standard to mark everything of value against.

GOOSE

—

THE GOOSE THAT LAYS THE GOLDEN EGGS

This goes back to fairy tales. The Goose appears in Aesop's fables as well as in many stories from around the world. She's a bird that regularly lays golden eggs. However, the owners of the goose believe she must have a large lump of gold inside her and so they kill her, and, of course, then there are no more golden eggs. The moral of the tale is, don't lose out on everything in a bid to sate short-term greed and desires.

GORILLA

A Gorilla company is one that has the biggest market share of its industry but doesn't necessarily have a monopoly. However, the size of its share means it is more able to take risks without fearing it will lose a significant customer base.

Furthermore, owing to its dominance of the market, the company exerts a great deal of control and influence. It can price competitively and often forces the competition to find alternative tactics in order to compete. In the 1990s Microsoft showed its mighty weight as a gorilla in the operating systems market.

GUINEA PIG

—

A Guinea Pig is another name for a test subject. Many people offer themselves up to be Guinea Pigs and will trial a new product in return for some sort of cash reward.

GUINEA PIG DIRECTOR

This goes back to the late nineteenth century and is a derogatory name for someone who, in financial journalist A.J. Wilson's glossary of stock market terms: 'lives by getting himself placed upon the Boards of a number of companies whose business he can have neither the time nor the qualifications to assist in directing'. The name came from the fact that this role would earn him the fee of one guinea; hence Guinea Pig Director.

These days, it's very common for companies to play host to non-executive directors – those who sit on the board but who don't get involved with management.

HAMSTER
——

HAMSTERKAUF

In 2020, the world came to an unexpected standstill as Covid-19, a new strain of coronavirus, took hold. Countries were put in lockdown, travel restrictions implemented and self-isolation measures put in place.

Despite attempts by governments to urge people to stay calm, customers seeking to stockpile led to a surge in demand for toilet roll, pasta and hand gel, among other commodities. This also meant that Hamsterkauf, a popular German word which translates to 'hamster purchase' came to the attention of the world.

It's a word that represents panic buying and a rise in Google searches and instances of its use on Twitter show that's just what was happening.

People were posting images of empty supermarket shelves and using the German phrase as a hashtag to comment on the trend. Hamsters love to hoard food in their cheek pouches, but with even pet food running out, there were concerns about the ramifications these stockpiling 'Hamsters' were doing to global supply chains.

HIPPO

—

Hippos might be bulky but they are also surprisingly graceful underwater and fast when on land. However, in the world of business, HIPPO is an acronym standing for the Highest Paid Person's Opinion and references the creature's slightly scary side.

Businesses should be wary of the HIPPO as, if it's allowed to dominate meetings and overrule over people's good ideas, it leads to a negative style of management and there's the potential for bad decisions to occur.

HORSE

—

GIFT HORSE

The expression goes, 'never look a gift horse in the mouth'. It sounds strange but there's a simple explanation. In the horse trade, prospective buyers would intently examine a horse's teeth in order to determine its age. Therefore, a gift shouldn't be treated with such mistrust and suspicion and simple requires a 'thank you'.

HORSE TRADING

Horse Trading is when a business deal is negotiated in a very forceful way, with all parties trying to get as much as they can. When the US internet publisher Gawker was put up for auction after filing for bankruptcy in 2016, there were over a dozen companies interested in buying, which resulted in much Horse Trading.

STALKING-HORSE

A Stalking-Horse refers to an early takeover bid on a distressed company (often one undergoing bankruptcy). Sometimes distressed companies will work in partnership with a stalking-horse bidder to test the market to see what the minimum acceptable price could be.

IBEX
—

IBEX 35

Not only is an ibex a type of wild mountain goat, it's also an acronym for the Spanish stock exchange. The Ibex 35 represents the thirty-five leading shares traded on the Madrid Stock Exchange General Index. It has been in operation since January 1992 and is reviewed twice a year.

KANGAROO

KANGAROO BONDS

Unsurprisingly, Kangaroo Bonds have an Australian link. Also known as Matilda Bonds, they are denominated in Australian dollars but are issued by foreign entities in the country.

In recent years the World Bank has been issuing Kangaroo bonds – even pricing up at least one based on blockchain (the technology underpinning digital currencies).

(See also Bulldog, Dragon, Kiwi and Panda Bonds, pp. 48, 54, 88 and 116.)

VAMPIRE KANGAROO

Meanwhile, maybe in a nod to the infamous Vampire Squid label given to Goldman Sachs (see p. 142), Australia's Macquarie Bank has been dubbed the Vampire Kangaroo by some in the UK. That's because of its involvement in private equity infrastructure deals and perceived ruthlessness when it comes to making a profit.

KIWI BONDS

The Kiwi bird is the national symbol of New Zealand and is a flightless bird. Kiwi bonds can only be bought by people resident in New Zealand. They are denominated in New Zealand dollars, with a fixed interest rate that is paid quarterly, in arrears. (See also Bulldog, Dragon, Kangaroo and Panda Bonds, pp.48, 54, 86 and 116.)

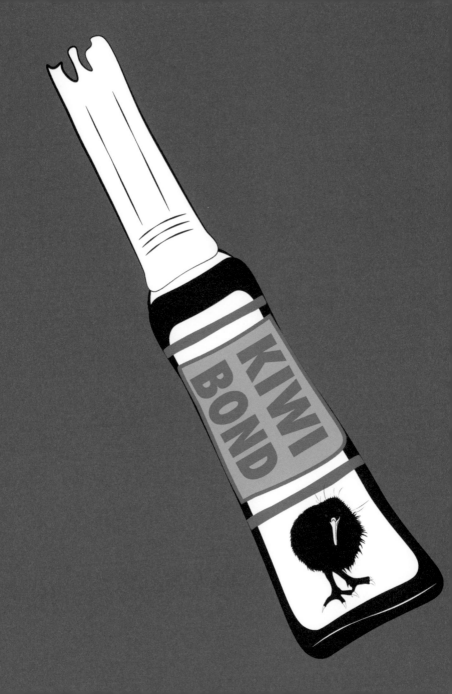

LEECH

—

As well as being a type of worm with suckers, a Leech also marks somebody out as the type of person who sponges off other people. They drain your money and have to be carefully removed. Steer clear or there might be nothing left of you...

LEMMING

—

A lemming is a small short-tailed rodent and the myth goes that they kill themselves through mass drownings.

They don't, by the way. But their population does boom every three or so years and so groups are sometimes forced into mass dispersals.

Anyway, the myth is too irresistible as a metaphor for describing human behaviour, and so, a Lemming investor is one who blindly follows the crowd without doing any of their own independent research. Needless to say, this can have negative consequences.

LION

—

LION ECONOMIES

This is a collective term, first used by Boston Consulting Group, to describe the eight main countries that are driving growth on the African continent: South Africa, Algeria, Botswana, Egypt, Mauritius, Libya, Morocco and Tunisia. However, it is also often used to refer to any African economy.

The lions have, on occasion, been described as 'sleeping', 'roaring' and conducting various other leonine behaviours. Either way, the markets are keeping a close eye on them.

LION'S SHARE

Of course you want to be careful near a lion – it is an apex land predator. But, at the same time, if someone offers you the lion's share, think twice before you turn that opportunity down. The lion gets the largest portion. The idiom is often associated with Ancient Greek storyteller Aesop and his famous fables but the idea of a lion's share turns up in eastern fables too. A story in the ancient Indian Jataka collection uses otters and jackals rather than lions.

LOBSTER

LOBSTER TRAP

Snap! A Lobster Trap is a defence strategy that a company
will deploy in order to prevent a hostile takeover. It will
pass a provision that stops anyone with more than ten
per cent ownership in the company from converting any
securities (such as bonds and stock, which would normally be
convertible) that would give additional voting rights.

LOBSTER SHIFT

If you like your sleep, then the lobster shift, also known as
the lobster trick, is not for you. The shift was given to those
working on overnights in the newspaper industry, although
the term has slipped into other fields. New York's *Daily
News* veteran photographer Charles Ruppmann revealed
that the name, for his organisation at least, originally came
from the fact that the antisocial shifts tallied with the time
that lobsters came into a nearby fish market. Much like a
rare albino lobster, it's actually quite hard to track down a
definitive origin story.

MEERKAT

—

THE MEERKAT EFFECT

Meerkats, with their keen sense of smell, vision and hearing, are often seen standing on their hind legs, vigilant to any danger. And there's a certain type of investor who behaves in the same way. They keep checking their financial portfolios and are hyper-alert when it comes to sniffing out information, especially when market conditions are changing.

This behaviour was first identified by researchers (Gherzi et al., 2014) who studied Barclays Wealth and Investment Management clients over a six year period. Their study refuted what was previously observed as the 'Ostrich Effect' (see p.112), which was seen as the investor's avoidance of negative financial information in the event of a downturn.

The Gherzi study identified a contrasting reaction and showed investors 'increasing their portfolio monitoring following both positive and negative daily market returns'. In this way, they more resemble hyper-vigilant meerkats than head-in-sand ostriches.

MOLES

A mole can refer to a blemish on your skin but, in business, it's something (or someone) you really want to watch out for.

Businesses might hire a Mole to find out what a competitor is up to. If you want to ensure your trade secrets stay safe, then make sure to root out any moles that might have tunnelled deep into your company.

MONKEY

—

CHIMP PARADOX

Personal development is a buzzword in the corporate world these days and Professor Steve Peters taps into this market with his idea of the Chimp Paradox. His theory focuses on our inner primate, which he sees as an emotional creature, thinking and acting without the say-so of our more rational 'human' consciousness.

Peters says that, if firms and individuals don't invest in emotional skills, there is a danger that an employee's 'chimp' might inadvertently go into 'catastrophe mode' and sabotage things in times of high stress.

MONKEY BUSINESS

Monkey Business is all about mischief making, something to be wary of in the financial world, unless this type of activity is what your business profits from.

We should note that, in the early 2000s, Yale economist Keith Chen and his colleagues Venkat Lakshminarayanan and Laurie R. Santos investigated if it were possible to teach monkeys (in this case Capuchins) how to trade. The researchers also looked at the risks the monkeys were willing to take and it showed how they were innately loss-averse, in the same way as humans.

Yes we know we've got chimps here playing and yes, we know they're actually apes, but we thought we'd indulge in a little bit of monkey business ourselves...

MOUSE

MOUSE POTATO

The term Mouse Potato first emerged in the 1990s.
It derives from the term couch potato as, while the latter
slobs in front of the TV, the former spends a lot of their time
click, click, clicking on the computer and staying at their
workstation. Either way, a sedentary lifestyle is the path
that's taken and isn't to be recommended.

NARWHAL

—

NARWHAL

A Canadian tech startup valued at more than $1 billion Canadian dollars and which was founded after 1999 can be described as a Narwhal. The term was coined by Brent Holliday, CEO of Vancouver company Garibaldi Capital Advisors. He chose the name as he 'understood the narwhal's horn was to break through the ice because they're mammals and have to breathe, so that's a great metaphor'. The tusks actually seem to be for sensory purposes but Holliday dismissed that and preferred to keep the original term. It has now gained wider usage and is often seen as a mascot for Canada's best performing companies – a unicorn of the sea (see p.158).

NEST EGG

A nice little (big) Nest Egg is what everybody wants to have when they retire as it means they've saved up enough money to live in a comfortable manner.

The phrase is believed to have originated with poultry farmers, who would drop an additional egg (both real and fake) into a hen's nest to try to induce her to produce even more. That way their own 'nest egg' would grow...

OSTRICH
—

THE OSTRICH EFFECT

The Ostrich Effect is a term from behavioural economics and was coined in a study by Dan Galai and Orly Sade. They observed the behaviour of investors and concluded that they monitored their portfolios more frequently in rising markets than when markets are falling.

The definition was further expanded by Niklas Karlsson, George Loewenstein and Duane J. Seppi who used it to mean 'avoiding exposing oneself to information that one fear may cause psychological discomfort'. Clearly then, avoiding the financial news would be a symptom of this.

However, ostriches don't, in fact, bury their heads in the sand as this would mean they were unable to breathe. What they do is dig holes in the dirt to use as nests for their eggs and so, several times a day, the mother ostrich buries her head in the hole and turns the eggs. Similarly, a more recent study has shown investors to more resemble the hyper-vigilant meerkat (see p. 98) rather than the head-down ostrich. Which one are you?

OWL

INVESTMENTS

OWL

—

Owls mark yet another type of investor behaviour. Identified in a report by SEI Private Wealth Management and Scorpio Partnership, they seem to fit in-between bullish and bearish behaviour.

'Owls are consultative and self-assured, yet reflective. They're pragmatic but open-minded. They're responsive yet realistic'.

PANDAS

PANDA BONDS

These are Chinese renminbi-denominated securities issued in the People's Republic of China by foreign borrowers. (See also Bulldog, Dragon, Kangaroo and Kiwi Bonds, pp. 48, 54, 86 and 88.)

PANDA DIPLOMACY

Did you know that China rents pandas out to zoos around the world? The creatures are big business for the country, and the resulting Panda Diplomacy has proved key to maintaining good relationships internationally.

An Oxford University study discovered that there are distinct stages to the history of panda diplomacy. These panda loans are now 'associated with nations supplying China with valuable resources and technology and symbolise China's willingness to build guanxi – namely, deep trade relationships characterised by trust, reciprocity, loyalty and longevity'.

PIGS

—

Pigs unfortunately have a reputation for being very greedy and so a Pig is any investor who gets so overexcited by the thought of profits that they lose sight of their original investment strategy for all the dollar signs in their eyes.

Sadly, the dreamed-of gains rarely tumble into their laps. In fact, there is a saying on Wall Street: 'Bulls make money, bears make money, pigs get slaughtered'.

PIGGY BANK

You might have had one of these in your childhood, for putting your spare change and pocket money in. In fact, the Piggy Bank has a very long history, going back to at least 1450. Before there were banks, people would stash their money at home in an earthenware pot called a 'pygg'. This explains why potters in the nineteenth century fashioned Piggy Banks after this farmyard animal. Oink.

PORK BARREL POLITICS

If we stay with the swine theme but just swivel slightly, Pork Barrel Politics appears in the political sphere. This refers to politicians being allocated federal government spending for particular projects in their regions as a means to help them garner political support.

PEACOCKS
—

A Peacock Market occurs when markets are overvalued and the stock valuations are inflated by central bank policy. The phrase suggests lots of showy display but, sadly, very little substance.

The term emerged in 2016, thanks to financial service company Hargreaves Lansdown, who warned at the time of various factors making investors feeling rather 'cagey'.

PORCUPINE

PORCUPINE PROVISION

A Porcupine Provision is a clause in a corporation's charter or bylaws to prevent a hostile takeover bid. It's a prickly way of stopping others from coming in and shaking up or destroying a company. (Also see Shark Repellents, p. 130).

PUMAS

—

PACIFIC PUMAS

This is another collective term, this time to describe the emerging economies of Latin America, which make up the Pacific Alliance. It was coined by financial adviser Samuel George of Bertelsmann Foundation and refers to Chile, Colombia, Mexico and Peru.

In 2014, George stated: 'Like the animal, these Pacific Pumas are comfortable operating quietly, away from the spotlight'.

RABBIT

BUNNY MARKET

Sometimes a market doesn't just go up or down. Sometimes, it hops like a... yes, you guessed it, bunny. Jim Paulsen, chief investment strategist at The Leuthold Group, first suggested the idea of a Bunny Market in a report to clients:

'Unlike an enthusiastic bull or a scary bear, a bunny market hops about a bit but really doesn't go anywhere, and bunnies have often dominated the stock market during the latter stages of past economic recoveries'.

RAT

RAT RACE

No-one really wants to think of themselves as a rat – an opportunistic rodent that swarms around in large packs. And so it is that many people try to escape the Rat Race once they realise they're in it. It refers to the constant struggle of urban life and competing to be successful but without necessarily finding the meaning of life.

RHINO

—

GREY RHINO

Beware the Grey Rhino as this large beast, according to the BBC's business correspondent Karishma Vaswani, 'refers to large, visible problems in an economy which are often ignored – until they start moving fast and trampling everything in their wake.'

Grey rhinos have recently become an issue in the Chinese economy. Many of its corporate giants, who were considered untouchable for a long time, were growing very quickly and borrowing a lot of money and this situation wasn't financially viable for the country as a whole.

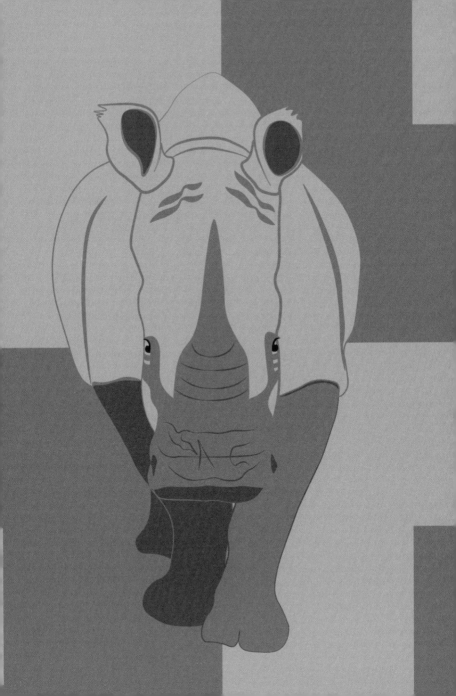

SHARKS
—

As sharks are predators who appear quite high up in the oceanic food chain, it's not surprising that they pop up time and time again in financial jargon – and it makes perfect sense for a company that's trying to execute a hostile takeover to be called a Shark.

LOAN SHARKS

If you can help it, try to stay away from loan sharks – a term for money lenders who charge extortionate interest rates.

SHARK REPELLENT

Sometimes the target company in a takeover bid will need to deploy a Shark Repellent to deter it. This could involve using any number of troublesome tactics, including negotiations, or a clause within the company's legal paperwork to make the target company seem less appealing. (See also, Porcupine Provision, p. 122.)

SHEEP

___

This term is another favourite of behavioural economists. A Sheep investor has no clear strategy and acts on their emotions or by listening to others, such as their friends or family (Also see Lemmings, p. 92).

Are they scared of making a baaa'd deal?

SKUNK

—

SKUNKWORKS PROJECT

A Skunkworks Project involves a small breakaway group of people in an organisation. Operating in a radical, unorthodox way, they hope to create something that will turn out to be rather special.

The name originally comes from Lockheed Martin's World War II Skunk Works ® group of American engineers who worked on advanced development projects, such as fighter jets. They had a lot of leeway and Kelly Johnson, who ran the original team, came up with fourteen strict rules about how the team should operate.

The name is now a registered trademark and yet the term is still used across businesses and the technology sector to refer informally to breakaway groups with their own autonomy. Both Amazon and Google are believed to have experimental labs operating in a skunkworks-like manner.

SNAKE

ANACONDA MORTGAGE

An Anaconda Mortgage is something that should make you wary of ever proceeding with buying a property without reading the smallprint.

This type of mortgage includes a particular clause (also known as a 'dragnet clause'), which is inserted by the lender, stating that the asset the loan is secured against (possibly your home) not only secures the debt originally intended but also any other future debts which might be owed.

In other words, the home is used as security for the original loan but then also for anything else. The mortgage lender could cheaply acquire the mortgagor's credit card debts, for example, and collect through the mortgage transaction. When their loans are called in, debtors find themselves in the coiled clutch of an anaconda, squeezed half to death. Ouch.

SNAKE IN THE TUNNEL

This was Europe's first attempt at monetary cooperation in the 1970s. Its aim was to limit fluctuations between different currencies and so the 'tunnel' was a band for currencies in the European Economic Community to operate in. Next came the European Monetary System in 1979, and the Euro in 1999.

SNAKES AND LADDERS

Snakes and Ladders is not just a board game for children. The *Oxford English Dictionary* describes it as 'a series of unpredictable successes and set-backs' and Nobel Prize-winning economist Professor Amartya Sen, has said the game is a useful way to understand the 'contemporary challenges of economic and social policies'.

SPIDER

MONEY SPIDER

The Money Spider is a tiny little spider, less than five millimeters in size, from a very large family. The scientific name of the family is *Linyphiidae* and there are 280 species within it but many cultures use the term 'money spider' to refer to all of them.

They spin huge sheet-like webbing, often in the garden as they like damp vegetation. The belief is that, if a money spider crawls on you or gets caught in your hair, you'll come into some kind of good fortune. Apparently, for extra good luck, you should spin the spider around your head by its web before you let it go.

SQUID

VAMPIRE SQUID

This expression came out of a famous *Rolling Stone* profile on Goldman Sachs, written by the journalist Matt Taibbi in 2009.

He said: 'The world's most powerful investment bank is a great vampire squid wrapped around the face of humanity, relentlessly jamming its blood funnel into anything that smells like money'.

He was writing in the context of the 2008 global financial crash and its aftermath but the label has stuck to the bank ever since.

SQUIRREL

PURPLE SQUIRREL

If you can find a purple squirrel, then my friend, you have something highly desirable in your sights.

The mythical rodent is, in recruiter circles, 'the perfect candidate'. They have every quality going that your business needs. They tick every box going: they have the right education, the right experience, the best attitude and the perfect qualifications. Ding, ding, ding – we have a winner.

However, while they might sound like a delight, critics warn that if rare purple squirrels ever get found, it's not necessarily good news for the rest of the workforce as it could mean fewer jobs are available. Also how on earth does this squirrel find time to keep across everything especially as roles evolve?

SWAN
—

BLACK SWAN EVENT

The former Wall Street trader, now scholar, statistician and essayist, Nassim Nicholas Taleb, came up with this famous motif.

Europeans once assumed all swans were white, until a black one was spotted in the southern hemisphere. Therefore, a Black Swan is a metaphor for an unpredictable high-impact event, such as the global financial crash of 2008.

The term has proved so influential that it has created spin-off labels, see below.

GREY SWAN EVENT

As grey is a mix of both black and white, a Grey Swan Event is high-impact and deemed unlikely, and yet anticipated 'to a certain degree'. The Japanese finance company Nomura, issues a yearly list of Grey Swan events and has previously suggested the following; the Chinese economy adopting a floating currency and the phasing out of paper money (with developed countries taking the lead on this).

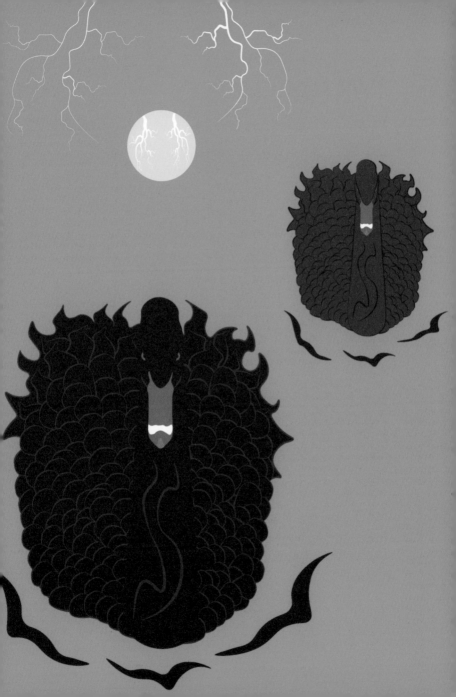

TIGER

—

ANATOLIAN TIGERS

This term is used to refer to a number of boom cities in central Turkey that have seen enormous industrial growth since the 1980s.

TIGER ECONOMY

This generic term can be applied to any economy that is growing rapidly along with a steep rise in living standards.

The original beasts are the Asian Tigers, so-called because tigers are central to these cultures – South Korea, Taiwan, Hong Kong and Singapore. However, Ireland has since had its Celtic Tiger, while Dubai is known as the Gulf Tiger and the Baltic Tigers refer to Lithuania, Latvia and Estonia.

TIGER CUB ECONOMIES

Now that the Southeast Asia economies of Indonesia, Malaysia, the Philippines, Thailand and Vietnam are chasing the heels of the original Asian Tigers, look out for the Cubs.

TOAD

JIN CHAN

Jin Chan translates literally as Golden Toad. It is also the name of a toad figurine with red eyes and three legs (only one hind leg), sitting on a pile of cash with a coin in its mouth. Similar to the Maneki-Neko (see p. 30), it is a wealth-beckoning lucky charm and is associated with Feng Shui – the Chinese art of being in harmony with the world around you.

This mythical creature is said to appear during the full moon near houses and businesses that will soon receive good news realting to their finances. Feng Shui beliefs hold that Jin Chan helps attract and protect wealth and guards against bad luck.

TORTOISE

TORTOISE RALLY

This term pays homage to Aesop's tale of the tortoise and the hare, where the slow but steady tortoise trumps the speedy but cocky hare. In the same way, a Tortoise Rally shows a slow but steady appreciation of market prices over time.

This isn't a place for volatility.

TURKEY

—

COLD TURKEY POLICY

A Cold Turkey Policy is when you try to rapidly reduce the inflation rate in a bid to meet a target. The other way to reduce it is to do so gradually. But if you go 'cold turkey', then there is a risk it could cause a deep recession. Policy makers have to decide whether they are reluctantly prepared to tolerate a sharp rise in unemployment to get inflation down quickly.

TURTLE

TURTLE TRADING

Turtle Trading stems back to a 1983 experiment carried out by high profile commodity traders Richard Dennis and Bill Eckhardt. They'd long been debating about how to become a successful trader. Dennis believed there was a formula while Eckhardt believed Dennis had a gift.

And so an experiment was devised, to settle the question of whether traders were born or taught. The term Turtles came about as Dennis remembered visiting a turtle farm in Singapore and set himself the challenge of creating proficient traders as quickly as the farm-bred turtles he had once seen grow.

The Turtles he picked, after placing an advertisement in *The Wall Street Journal*, learned how to watch trends and many went on to become high profile traders in their own right.

UNICORN

—

A Unicorn is, of course, a magical creature and so it's unsurprising that, in business, this name has been bestowed on startups that have grown in value from nothing to at least $1 billion US dollars.

The phrase was invented in 2013 by venture capitalist Aileen Lee. Famous Unicorns include Airbnb, Facebook and SpaceX and, while the term is now in common parlance, the number of true Unicorns remains in the hundreds, at the time of writing.

UNICORN BUBBLE

This is what happens when venture capitalists or investors overvalue a company, and it can occur during their private phase or at the point of their initial public offering.

WEASEL

WEASEL CLAUSE

This is an escape clause in a contract allowing one of the parties to 'weasel' their way out.

WHALE

WHALE WATCHING

This is the point on our animal safari when we sit back and watch the Whales – the big players and investors, such as Warren Buffett (see p. 62) – to see what move they will make next.

WHALE PROSPECT

Don't forget the scale of a whale – it's huge. In Business to Business sales, a Whale Prospect is a company that is far larger than your own.

WILDCAT

WILDCAT BANKING

This refers to the period between 1837 and 1865, when US banks were established in remote rural outposts, often where wildcats lived. They were chartered by individual state law but without any federal oversight. The period is also known as the Free Banking Era.

WILDCAT DRILLING

This is the term used for exploratory oil drilling, primarily by small operators.

WILDCAT STRIKES

Wildcat Strikes are carried out by union members but without the union's leadership necessarily approving or sometimes even knowing of it.

WOLF

WOLF ECONOMY

This is Mongolia's answer to the Asian Tiger economy (see p. 148). The wolf is revered in Mongolia and, with the country now extensively mining its rich mineral deposits, it sees itself as 'a wolf on the move', eyeing up a piece of the action for itself.

WOLF OF WALL STREET

This was the nickname originally given to the American financial investor, Jordan Belfort, who was, in his own words, 'a stock market millionaire at twenty-six and a federal convict at thirty-six'. He then used it as the title of his memoirs, which then became a film by Martin Scorsese, starring Leonardo DiCaprio.

However, Belfort wasn't the first 'Wolf of Wall Street'. In the early twentieth century a conman named David Lamar, who at one point pretended to be a US Senator, went by the same moniker. These days, a Wolf of Wall Street is the name given to any hungry investor who shimmies unscrupulously up the financial ladder.

YAK

—

YAK SHAVING

You're probably wondering if 'yak shaving' is a thing... Well yes, yak farmers often do shear their herd, although many choose to comb the hairs out (this wool is highly prized). However, in the world of business, yak shaving isn't quite so straightforward.

Student Carlin Vieri coined the term in the '90s after watching an episode of *The Ren and Stimpy Show* featuring 'Yak Shaving Day' – a day a little like Christmas but full of bizarre and random rituals. He then applied the term to programming, in reference to all the fiddly, seemingly inconsequential tasks that might appear tangential and useless to your main objective and yet which become a key part of the process in the grand scheme of things.

The phrase however has moved way beyond the lab and is now used when it comes to talking about focusing your energies on something tangential to what you were supposed to be doing in the first place. However, in the grand scheme of things – think bigger picture – those small tasks might look pointless at first but actually end up playing a causal role in the end result.

ZEBRA

——

ZEBRAS UNITE

In 2017, a new movement emerged in the Silicon Valley.

A group of entrepreneurs got together seeking to create a culture change in the Unicorn dominated tech scene. They called for more 'zebra' companies.

Zebras Unite became a call to action to get more funding for startups initiated by women and people from ethnic minorities and to balance the existing venture capital culture. The founders of the movement – Jennifer Brandel, Mara Zepeda, Astrid Scholz and Aniyia Williams – say this is 'a moral imperative' and that, 'unlike unicorns, zebras are real'.

They described Zebra companies as 'profitable businesses that solve real, meaningful problems and in the process repair existing social systems'.

The movement is now well established with chapters based all over the world. And of course, as a group of Zebras is known as a 'dazzle', the founders have, of course, used this collective noun as the name of their annual conference.

REFERENCES

Animal Spirits
John Maynard Keynes, *The General Theory of Employment, Interest and Money*, (London: Macmillan, 1936)

Ants
Gloria Cheung, 'China cracks down on 'financial ants' smuggling cash to Hong Kong', *Financial Times* (2 April, 2017), https://www.ft.com/content/6aa1faca-bd2e-11e6-8b45-b8b81dd5d080

Bird in the hand
M.J. Gordon, 'Dividends, Earnings, and Stock Prices', *The Review of Economics And Statistics*, 41 (2), (May, 1959), pp. 99–105, www.jstor.org/stable/1927792

Black swan
Nassim Nicholas Taleb, *The Black Swan: The Impact of the Highly Improbable*, (London: Allen Lane, 2007)

Boiled frog theory
Paul Krugman, 'Boiling the Frog', *The New York Times* (12 July 2009), https://www.nytimes.com/2009/07/13/opinion/13krugman.html

Bunny markets
James W. Paulson, 'A bull, a bear, or a bunny?', *Wells Capital Management Economic and Market Perspective* (21 March 2016), http://ig.cdn.responsys.net/i4/responsysimages/str2/__RS_CP_/20160322_EMP.pdf

Bulldog bonds
Andrew Walker, 'What are bonds and how do they work?', *BBC News* (13 September 2016), https://www.bbc.com/news/business-37175814

Chimp paradox
Dr Steve Peters, *The Chimp Paradox*, (London: Vermillion, 2012)

Civets
'BRICS and BICIS', *The Economist* (26 November 2009), https://www.economist.com/the-world-in-2010/2009/11/26/brics-and-bicis

Cockroaches
Dylan Grice, 'The Last Popular Delusions', Société General (23 November 2012), https://www.zerohedge.com/sites/default/files/images/user5/imageroot/2012/11/Dylan%20Grice%20-%20Goodbye.pdf
Caterina Fake, 'The Age of the Cockroach', Medium (30 September 2015), https://medium.com/@caterina/the-age-of-the-cockroach-5a720d917416

Dogecoin
'Dogecoin's $2 Billion Value: So High, Much Fall', *Bloomberg Daybreak: Australia* (22 January 2018), https://www.bloomberg.com/news/videos/2018-01-22/co-creator-palmer-says-dogecoin-should-remain-a-joke-video

Dogs of the dow
Michael B. O'Higgins and John Downes, *Beating the Dow Completely Revised and Updated*, (London: HarperCollins e-books, 2011)

Dragon kings

Didier Sornette, 'Dragon-Kings, Black Swans and the Prediction of Crises', *CCSS Working Paper*, No. CCSS-09-005 (24 July 2009), https://ssrn.com/abstract=1596032

Eagles

'EAGLEs Economic Outlook', BBVA Research, (accessed 7 October 2018), https://www.bbvaresearch.com/en/publicaciones/eagles-economic-outlook/

Elephant curve

Branko Milanovic, 'Global Income Inequality by the Numbers: in History and Now', The World Bank, (accessed 6 October 2018), p. 13, http://documents.worldbank.org/curated/en/959251468176687085/pdf/wps6259.pdf

Dylan Matthews, 'The Global Top 1 Percent Earned Twice as Much as the Bottom 50 percent in Recent Years', *Vox* (2 February 2008), https://www.vox.com/policy-and-politics/2018/2/2/16868838/elephant-graph-chart-global-inequality-economic-growth

Hunting the elephant

Dominc Lawson, Robert Peston and Grant Ringshaw, 'Warren Buffett: My elephant gun is loaded', *The Sunday Telegraph* (22 September 2002), https://www.telegraph.co.uk/finance/personalfinance/investing/shares/2774088/Warren-Buffett-My-elephant-gun-is-loaded.html

Fat cat

Frank Kent, 'Fat Cats and Free Rides', *The American Mercury*, 14 (54) (June 1928), p. 130

Fishbone analysis

Kaoru Ishikawa, *Guide to Quality Control*, (Tokyo: Asian Productivity Organization, 1976)

Flea market

George S. Dougherty, *In Europe*, (New York: Pusey Press, 1922)

Gazelles

David L. Birch, Anne Haggerty and William Parsons, *Who's Creating Jobs?*, (Cambridge: Cognetics, Inc.,1995)

Grey rhino

Karishma Vaswani, 'Hunting rhinos: What Dalian Wanda saga says about China', *BBC News* (26 July 2017), https://www.bbc.co.uk/news/business-40714515

Grey swan

Bilal Hafeez, Andy Cates, Jordan Rochester, Andy Chaytor, 10 Grey Swan Events for 2018, Nomura Connects, (December 2017) https://web.archive.org/web/20180519014808/http://www.nomuraconnects.com/focused-thinking-posts/10-grey-swan-events-for-2018/

Guinea pig director

A.J. Wilson, *A Glossary of Colloquial Slang and Technical Terms in use on the Stock Exchange and in the Money Market*, (London: Wilsons & Milne, 1985)

Lame duck

Horace Walpole, *The Letters of Horace Walpole, Fourth Earl of Orford: Volume 1*, (Philadelphia, Lea & Blanchard, 1844) p.40

Lion economies

Sami Chabenne, Patrick Dupoux, Lisa Ivers, David C. Michael, Yves Morieux, 'The African Challengers: Global Competitors Emerge from the Overlooked Continent', The Boston Consultancy Group (May 2010), https://image-src.bcg.com/Images/BCG_The_African_Challengers_May_2010_tcm9-119545.pdf

Meerkat effect

Svetlana Gherzi, Daniel Egan, Neil Stewart, Emily Haisley and Peter Ayton, 'The Meerkat Effect: Personality and Market Returns Affect Investors' Portfolio Monitoring Behaviour', *Journal of Economic Behavior & Organization*, 107 (2014), pp. 512–526, http://wrap.warwick.ac.uk/66015/

Monkey business

M. Keith Chen, Venkat Lakshminarayanan, Laurie R. Santos, 'How Basic Are Behavioral Biases? Evidence from Capuchin Monkey Trading Behavior', *Journal of Political Economy*, 114 (3), (June 2003), pp. 517–537, https://www.journals.uchicago.edu/doi/abs/10.1086/503550

Narwhals

Alice Troung, 'Canadian Tech Unicorns are called Narwhals', *Quartz* (20 November 2015), https://qz.com/554928/canadian-tech-unicornsare-called-narwhals/

Ostrich effect

"The ostrich effect: Selective attention to information", Niklas Karlsson, Niklas, George Loewenstein, Duane Seppi, *Journal of Risk and Uncertainty*, 38, (11 February 2009), pp. 95–115, https://link.springer.com/article/10.1007/s11166-009-9060-6

Dan Galai, Orly Sade, 'The "Ostrich Effect" and the Relationship between the Liquidity and the Yields of Financial Assets', (July 2003), https://ssrn.com/abstract=431180

Owl

'Are you a bear, a bull or owl?' Presentation published by SEI.com (accessed May 2020), https://www.advisorselect.com/transcript/SEI/are-you-a-bear-bull-or-owl

Pacific pumas

Samuel George, 'The Pacific Pumas: An Emerging Model for Emerging Markets', Bertlesmann Foundation (13, March 2014), p. 130, https://www.bfna.org/wp-content/uploads/2017/04/The-Pacific_Pumas-Single-13Mar14.pdf

Panda diplomacy

Kathleen Carmel Buckingham, Jonathan Neil William David, Paul Jepson, 'Environmental reviews and case studies: Diplomats and Refugees: Panda Diplomacy, Soft "Cuddly" Power, and the New Trajectory in Panda Conservation', *Environmental Practice*, 15 (3), (2013), pp. 262–270, https://www.cambridge.org/core/journals/environmental-practice/article/environmental-reviews-and-case-studies-diplomats-and-refugees-panda-diplomacy-soft-cuddly-power-and-the-new-trajectory-in-panda-conservation/A23238335C47C1717417060B7AAB05AFA23238335C47C1717417060B7AAB05AF

Peacock

Investors wary of 'peacock market' as confidence hits record low, The Actuary, Seekings, Chris, 10, November, 2016, https://www.theactuary.com/news/2016/11/investors-wary-of-peacock-market-as-confidence-hits-record-low/

Queen bee

'Queen Bee' Stereotype in the Workplace is a Rarity, Today website, Langfield, Amy, 14, October 2016 https://www.today.com/money/queen-bee-stereotype-workplace-rarity-1C8768020

Red herring

The S.E.C and A Free Securities Market Address of Richard B. McEntire, Commissioner, Securities and Exchange Commission Before the Illinois Securities Dealers Association, 15, January 1947 https://www.sec.gov/news/speech/1947/011547mcentire.pdf

Sacred cow

A Business and Its Beliefs, Watson Jr, Tom, McGraw-Hill, 2003. e-text accessed on 06 October 2018 via https://bit.ly/2CtHaNo

Skunk Works

Skunk Works Origin Story, Lockheed Martin website, accessed 09, October, 2018 https://www.lockheedmartin.com/us/aeronautics/skunkworks/origin.html

Snakes and ladders

Snakes and Ladders, The Financial Times, Sen, Amartya, 23, December 2011 https://www.ft.com/content/f83e170c-4261-3854-be1d-8fa1c449a7bf

Turtle trading

Winning Commodity Traders May Be Made, Not Born, The Wall Street Journal, Angrist, Stanley, W, 5, September 1989

Ugly duckling stocks

Seeing the Beauty in Ugly-Duckling Stocks, Barrons, DeFotis, Dimitra, 8 May, 2012; https://www.barrons.com/articles/SB500014240531190393530457738196021423378

Unicorn

Welcome to the Unicorn Club: Learning from Billion Dollar Start-Ups, Techcrunch, Lee, Aileen, 02, November 2013, https://techcrunch.com/2013/11/02/welcome-to-the-unicorn-club/

Vampire kangaroo

Enter the Vampire Kangaroo, The Sunday Times, Fortson Danny, 10 February 2013, https://www.thetimes.co.uk/article/enter-the-vampire-kangaroo-rs62j9f2lc3, accessed 22 April 2020

Vampire squid

The Great American Bubble Machine, Rolling Stone, Taibbi, Matt, 05 April, 2010 https://www.rollingstone.com/politics/politics-news/the-great-american-bubble-machine-195229/

Vomiting camel

'Clear "vomiting camel" in RDX. My brilliant colleague's latest technical analysis :)', Tweet, Twitter, Platerink, Suvi, @Suvikosonen, 12, March 2014 https://twitter.com/suvikosonen/status/443752300503248896
The truth behind the vomiting camel graph, The Financial Times, Martin, Katie, 19, April 2018, https://www.ft.com/video/2452d265-ef0e-4f7f-b0b2-ca1dc076ff33

Wolf of Wall Street

'Wolf of Wall St' Held in Stock Fraud; The New York Times, 16, June 1932. Archive accessed on 09, Oct, 2018, https://www.nytimes.com/1932/06/16/archives/wolf-of-wall-st-held-in-stock-fraud-lamar-is-arrested-in-bennetts.html

Yak shavings

Jeremy H Brown email, MIT emails, 11 Feb 2000, http://projects.csail.mit.edu/gsb/old-archive/gsb-archive/gsb2000-02-11.html

Zebra

Zebras Fix What Unicorns Break, Medium, Brandel Jennifer, Zepeda Mara, Astrid Scholz Astrid, & Williams Aniyia, 8 March 2017, https://medium.com/@sexandstartups/zebrasfix-c467e55f9d96

INDEX

ACKNOWLEDGEMENTS

We're especially grateful to those people who believed in our idea from the very beginning and helped it to grow.

Dominic wishes to thank Lucy, Luke and Jake for their support, while Dhruti wants to say thank you to the wonderful Shah family – Chandrakant, Nalina, Gemini, Sapna, Minesh, Rian and Rahi Tulsi.

With additional thanks to business experts Andrew Walker, Ameer Khan, Russ Mould, Kim Gittleson, Lucy Burton, Laurence Knight, Frey Lindsay, Gemma Holmes, Joe Miller, Phil Macartney, Szu Ping Chan, Travis Burke, Darsan Shah and Mayur Shah for helping us to hone our definitions, and to Lucinda Rumsey whose copy of the original *Medieval Bestiary* has been a guiding force.

Of course, to create such a compendium, we've had to spend a lot of time digging through a plethora of historical records and market reports. The *Oxford English Dictionary* has been invaluable, as have the *Financial Times*, *Forbes*, *Investopedia*, *Wikipedia*, Twitter conversations, and the expertise of the BBC's Business Unit.

Please note illustrations for thirty of these beasts were first published on the 'A-Z Guide to Business Beasts' (also created by the authors of this book) and can be found at www.bbc.com/businessbeasts

We also want to say thank you to all our friends at the BBC and beyond, and also to Polly Powell, David Graham, Lucy Smith and Cara Armstrong at Pavilion who supported and guided us through this endeavour.